BOD
THE BEAST OF BODMIN MOOR

BOD

THE BEAST OF BODMIN MOOR

A TRIBUTE TO THE BEAST OF BODMIN MOOR

Endymion Beer

HALSGROVE

First published in Great Britain in 2006

British Library Cataloguing-in-Publication Data
A CIP record for this title is available from the British Library

ISBN 1 84114 574 2   •   ISBN 978 1 84114 574 7

HALSGROVE
Halsgrove House
Lower Moor Way
Tiverton, Devon EX16 6SS
Tel: 01884 243242
Fax: 01884 243325
email: sales@halsgrove.com
website: www.halsgrove.com

Printed and bound by The Cromwell Press, Trowbridge

The cover image is from an original oil painting by Trevor Beer, courtesy of Mrs Bradley

Dedication

To Robin and Rosemary,
with thanks to Trevor
and greetings to Karl.

Foreword

The so-called 'Beast' of Bodmin Big Cat is actually a number of feral big cats including black leopard and puma inhabiting Bodmin Moor and the wilds of Cornwall. It is like the Dartmoor and Exmoor big cat phenomenon a true story based on escapes and releases from captive situations over many years. Breeding has occurred and thus we have feral big cats due to humans with no blame to be attached to the cats. They live secluded lives, finding food and shelter where they can and will not harm humans unless disturbed and pressured. So, leave them alone.

Many pumas and other 'exotic' cat species including black leopards were suddenly 'in the wild' following the Dangerous Wild Animals Act. 1976. Tougher controls and some legislation led to some 'pet owners' being put into a situation of releasing or putting down their 'friends'. As two or three big-cat owners said to me, "when you are emotionally involved with your animals which way do you go?" Thereby hangs a tale, or tail.

I am therefore honoured and pleased as one who has been observing and investigating the natural history of these animals in Britain for many years, to write this foreword for my friend and colleague's book on the exploits of Bod and Min in the Westcountry. The story boards are amusing and informative, placing the cats in real places in a pleasing and light-hearted manner. The animals fully deserve a 'good press' and thanks to Endymion here it is.

Trevor Beer MBE
North Devon 2006

The beginning...

Bod – The Beast of Bodmin

Bod finds himself on Bodmin Moor but who is going to feed him? Ah me! He'll have to learn to hunt for himself now he's escaped from his captors.

With ears back, he tries to creep up on his prey.

But the rabbits are too smart and the pheasant too noisy!

Thank goodness for the absent minded farmer. Bod says his sandwiches tasted grrrrreat!

The news on the radio tells Bod police are looking for another Big-Cat recently escaped from a zoo!

A lady reported a Big-Cat sighting and police rushed to the scene.

But it was only a black bin liner stuffed in the hedge. All a case of misidentification. Oh dear.

Or was it? For on the other side of the hedge Bod is drinking from a puddle, wondering if he'll get to meet the new Big-Cat.

Bod was looking at his reflection in a puddle.

He decided no beast was more handsome!

Suddenly Bod grows another head. Oh dear!

"My name is Min, I'm the escaped Big-Cat from the zoo." Says the other head. Bod is relieved not to have grown two heads.

Together Bod and Min are finding their way around Britain. Don't forget Britain is a foreign country to them.

"The climate is different." Says Bod. "The food is different too." Says Min.

"And the moorland isn't a bit jungle-like." Bod complains.

"But at least it's the same sun that shines above us and the same lovely moon at night." Says Min. How romantic!

Bod and his new companion, Min, are getting on well. First they had a good wash...

...then shared a meal. They ate everything up. (High in a tree)

They didn't eat with their mouths open. (So sucked most of it.)

Finally they made T in their muddy habitat as they'd heard that's what the people of Britain generally do.

Bod is being an utter toad.

So Min takes him off for a walk… er… backwards.

Lots of fungi about. Bod likes the one called Panther Cap. It's poisonous but like Bod says, not everything is for eating.

Min's favourite is the toadstool.

Bod and Min can't sleep.

Lots of spooky noises outside their lair.

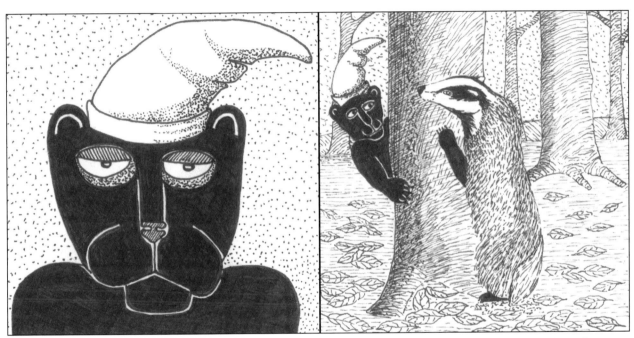

Bod ventures outside to investigate.

But all is well. It's only badger badgering about.

It's a lovely misty morning. Bod and Min discover an apple tree.

Bod and Min like the look of the over ripe apples but neither eat apples of course.

What will they do with them? Well, Bod decides to juggle them so Min stands well out of the way.

Then they have a better idea and play apple marbles instead. What fun!

It's Halloween! Min is trying her paw at apple bobbing. Bod isn't exactly helping.

As night falls, two spooky ghosts appear. Oh my!

The ghosts are making people and animals jump out of their skins!

But all is well. It's only Bod and Min dressed up.

Bod and Min are off to make a Cat Fawkes for Bonfire Night.

Min fetches some hay from the farmer's barn. She'll use this for stuffing.

Bod borrows some washing. Oops! 5 socks and 1 pillowcase.

Bod and Min set to work to make their Cat Fawkes. They think its grrrrrreat!

Colliford Lake is frozen. Brrrr!

Min is ice-skating with squirrel.

Bod is trying his paw at skiing but he's already in trouble! Look out Bod!

Now how did he do that! What a cool cat Bod is!

Bod and Min like the way that snow crunches under their paws.

As the snow falls harder, they decide to make a Snow-Bod. "There's snow place like home." Laughs Bod.

"Look Min, it's Otter!" Cries Bod, pleased to see Otter running through the snowy landscape.

"Brrr… No I'm colder today, not hotter." Giggles Min. Ah me!

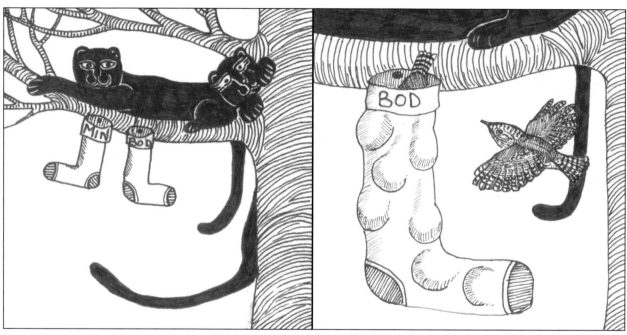

It's Christmas Eve. Bod and Min are hanging up their stockings before bedtime.

But it's such a cold night that 9 little wrens decide to roost in Bod's Stocking…

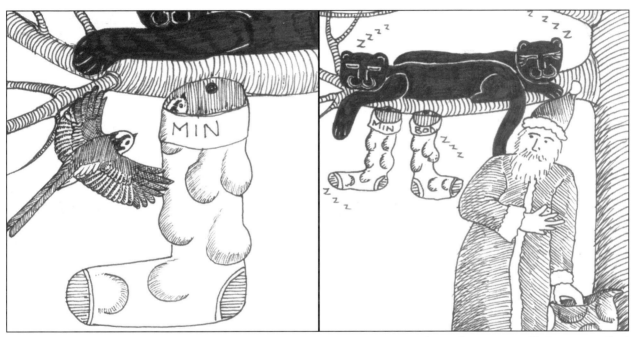

...and 8 long-tailed tits decide to roost in Min's stocking.

Well, now Father Christmas will have to find another place to put the presents.

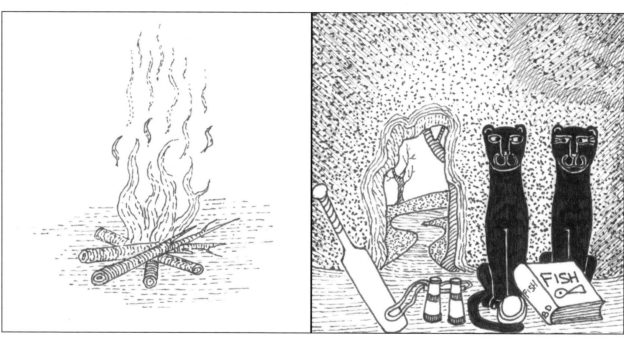

Min has kept a fire burning throughout New Year's Eve for luck.

She and Bod plan what to do when the clock strikes midnight since in folklore, that's what they'll be doing all the following year.

What a surprise. They decide to eat a big chicken. Min hopes her First New Year visitor will be tall, dark and male for luck.

Sure enough her visitor fits the description. He brings a piece of coal for the fire and walks out again in silence. Now who could that have been?

Min will need her own hunting territory soon. Bod has agreed to help her find a place of her own.

And so it is that Bod and Min go around and about searching for a while.

First they arrive at Trethevy Quoit, one of the most impressive monuments in Britain.

Min says it's 'quoit' nice. Bod chuckles. They'll continue to look around and about though.

"So this is King Doniert's stone and cross." Exclaims Min.

"Yes, but of course he was really King Bod, one of my Ancestors." Fibs Bod. Luckily Min doesn't believe him.

Suddenly Merlin materialises before them in a white mist. He has a secret for them. He says…

"Dungarth (Doniert) ordered this cross to save King Arthur's soul but was drowned by Mordred's knights for liaison with Arthur, King of Britain." Merlin vanishes.

Brown Willy, the highest point on Bodmin Moor and a wild place to explore.

Bod and Min have a take-a-way. Bod takes a pheasant. Min takes a rabbit. They have a picnic.

"That was a very pheasant meal." Grins Min. "Stop rabbitting on." Teases Bod.

"You know we're not native to this country but, nor are rabbits and pheasants. We're all aliens really." Says Bod.

Bod and Min are sniffing around Jamacia Inn on a moon-lit winter's night.

"Min, this place is haunted." Says Bod. "We'll make a cross for protection." Announces Min.

Just then a ghost appears. "Quick show your cross." Shouts Bod.

"Shove off you rotten so and so!" Shouts Min. I don't think that's quite what Bod meant.

Degu is on holiday at Tintagel. Bod and Min are coming to pick him up.

Degu wants to show Bod and Min Merlin's Cave before going home.

So they venture down to the beach. The tide is out and it's a lovely day... Ah me!

To their great surprise Merlin the Magician is at home in his cave. He invites them all to tea.

Bod and Min find a lunch box by Dozmary Pool but neither of them like the contents.

Bod is furiously disappointed and tosses it into the lake.

Min thinks that was a dreadful thing to do and tells Bod so.

But all is well. The Lady of the Lake catches it. She hasn't eaten for centuries!

Oh no the goats have escaped! They're on a rampage eating all the flowers across Cornwall!

They gallop about for miles to eventually end up at Lanhydrock! What will the National Trust say!

The pygmy goats hide in the gardens nibbling at this plant and that shrub. They're going to be in so much trouble!

But all is well for this time it's Min to the rescue. Hooray. She rounds them up and takes them home for a talking to. Ooops!

The Vietnamese Pot-Bellied piglet, called P.B for short, is being rude. He's stuck his tongue out to all the animals at Colliford Lake.

In fact the animals are so fed up with his rudeness, they decide to put him in Bodmin Jail to teach him a lesson.

Bod says that was a bit harsh. He's going to rescue P.B.

P.B is so glad to be free again! He promises never to poke his tongue out again.

Bod and Min are prowling around and about. They Contemplate some art At Dobwalls Family Adventure Park…

Then lurk in the shadows at Carnglaze Caverns so as not to be seen (in case they're caught and sent to a zoo.)

They ride on a fun train at Bodmin and Wenford Railway. Wheee!

They end up resting at Restormel Castle before legging it home in time for tea. What an exciting day!

"Hey Bod, what are all these stones?" Asks Min.

Bod tells her they're The Hurlers, reckoned to be two teams playing hurlers on a Sunday and thus turned to stone.

"How do you play Hurlers?" Min wants to know.
"It's a rough stick and ball game like this." Bod
demonstrates.

Min pleads Bod to stop because it's Sunday but Bod
says "Ah, rubbish!" Oh dear now he's in trouble –
as usual.

Min read somewhere that drinking the water at St Cleer's Well cures madness.

Bod and Min visit St Cleer to investigate...

"Well Bod, you're the nutty one so you drink the water first. Let's see if it works." Says Min.

Bod laps some of the water. Oh dear, it hasn't worked!

The Vietnamese Pot-Bellied pig (P.B) has hurt his trotter. "Oh ouch!" He grumbles.

Bod takes P.B to the village of St Neot for some oinkment, er, I mean ointment.

But when they arrive it's dark. St Neot himself is waiting for them! He's a tiny Saint but wonderful with animals.

St Neot heals P.B. Hooray! Now Bod and P.B can trot off home. Thanks St Neot.

"St Neot's Holy Well. Hmmm let's investigate." Says Bod.

"Holy Well. Cor! It's only got one hole in it." Says Min.

"No silly Holy as in a special place of St Neot. Not as in lots of holes." Giggles Bod.

"I like it here. Let's stay the night in peace. Good night Min" Sighs Bod.

"Cornish Country Meats" near St.Neot have a job vacancy.

Bod and Min can not resist. They're going to apply. "We must go disguised." Bod tells Min.

At the interview Min says she wants to be a taster. Bod tries his paw at packing but dribbles everywhere.

Luckily neither get the job so they can't eat everything after all...

Min finds a book on Egypt a school party left behind.

"Doesn't the sphinx look deep in thought." She says to Bod.

"I expect it's thinking magical and mysterious thoughts." Announces Fox who happens to be running by.

"No Fox, it's 'sphinking' magical and mysterious thoughts." Laughs Bod.

Bod and Min meet Kia the pussy cat curator at The Ancient Egyptian Centre.

Kia is extremely acrobatic. She shows Bod and Min around.

Their favourite statue is the one of Bast with the blue back light. Ah me!

After enjoying the Edwards and Beilby collection, they all dance like Egyptians. Grrrreat!

Bod and Min visit Golitha Falls.

Bod is skimming pebbles in the water.

"Ouch!" Yelps Min as a pebble catches her ankle. Ooops!

"Bod, it's supposed to be Golitha Falls, it's not supposed to be David and Goliath." Min Tells Bod. But all is well.

Bod and Min visit Siblyback Reservoir.

They're having a go at canoeing.

Unfortunately they enjoy splashing each other far better and soon capsize!

Luckily they are good swimmers and are soon safely ashore.

Bod has gone off for a quiet spot of fishing between St Austell Bay and Fowey.

It isn't long before he gets a bite.

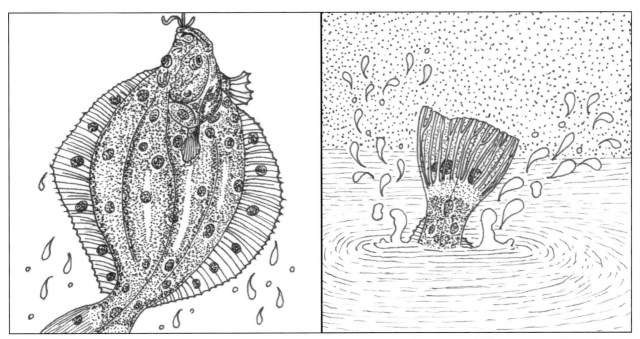

He reels in a lovely big plaice but, it wriggles free!

"There's no plaice (place) like home, Bod." Cries out the fish before escaping!

Today is Valentine's Day. Bod hates mush!

All the birds are pairing up. Min thinks it's *so* romantic. She's got something to tell Bod and goes off to find him.

"Since rabbits and pheasants seem to be on the increase Bod, I don't need my own hunting grounds after all. So we can stop searching around and about. She tells him.

Well, Bod is delighted!   Min has chosen to stay. "Happy Valentine's Day!" They say in unison. Ahh!

Bod and Min have become proper twitchers. They love bird watching.

Min spots a crow with red legs and beak.

Bod tells her it's a Chough, Cornwall's County bird.

Min says... "Well I'm certainly chuffed to see it!"
Ah me!

"Come on Min, let's go for a walk." Bod says.

Soon they find a strange plant." "What is it Min?" Min is good at plants.

"Oh it's a Parson in the Pulpit." She tells Him, using the country name for Wild Arum.

"No…" says Bod, "… I think he's just out for a walk like us."

It's Easter! Colliford Lake Park is officially open for visitors.

Bod and Min are busy hiding Easter eggs for their friends to find.

Soon all the eggs are found but Bod and Min are left out. Oh dear!

But all is well. Grass Snake gives them one of hers. Oops! It's hatched!

Today the farmer's hat blew right off! Bod found it.   Min says, "Bod there's a whee in your hat!"

Bod is horrified! "What!" He cries. "Oh yes." Says Min grabbing the hat.

"Look… wheeee!" She cries tossing the hat back to the farmer.

Min is sure Bod wont forget it's her birthday but baby squirrel isn't so sure.

Bod is too busy making rabbit pooh and mud pies to remember anything.

Finally a little bird has to remind Bod.

Bod fetches a delicious chop for Min's present. Her favourite!

continued overleaf

The trouble is the scent overwhelms him and... Oh no Bod... No don't!

Too late he's eaten it.

Now what will he do? Min is approaching and Bod has no gift for her.

Bod is such a cool cat. He picks her flowers instead. Phew!

Today is Bod's birthday, although none of the animals at Colliford Lake Park have remembered!

Even worse, the birds are chirping behind his back.

The animals don't want Bod listening to them either.

But all is well. They've been planning a surprise birthday party. Bod is delighted!

continued overleaf

Min is bringing Bod a present.

Bod hopes he gets lots of presents!

He won't be disappointed all the birds and animals at Colliford Lake Park remembered him.

Min hopes Bod opens his presents nicely but Bod has a rrrrripping time!

Min can't understand how people can keep changing their fur...

Bod explains that people change their clothes. "They don't have any fur." He tells her.

Now Min thinks that's odd because all the animals she sees have fur. "Where do they get clothes?" She asks Bod. He tells her about shops and catalogues.

"Catalogues?... What like this?" Demonstrates Min giggling. "Well just so long as it isn't a dogalogue!" Laughs Bod.

NEW IMAGE
5000 new ladies styles and hardly any choice for men

Min was quite peacefully sitting in the meadow.

All of a sudden a voice says…"Two buttercups and five poppies makes seven wild flowers.

And then the voice says... "Three common blues and six gatekeepers makes nine butterflies."

"Who is it?" Calls Min. "It's me Min. I'm an adder." Replies the snake. Ah me!

Min is worried!

Bod has acquired a second tail. Oh my!

Further more, he doesn't seem a bit bothered by his new acquisition.

But all is well. Bod's second tail is merely grass snake basking in the sun. Phew!

Bod and Min are out for a walk.   They have a great time nosing around.

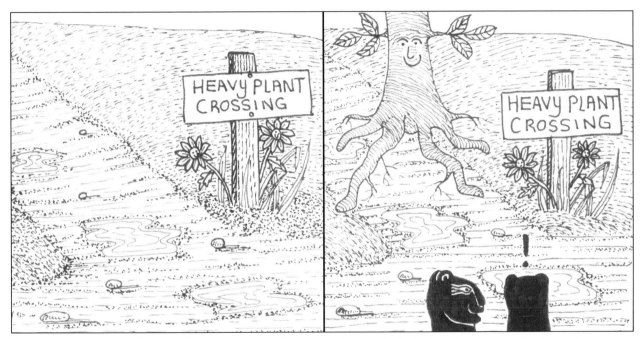

They come across a heavy plant crossing, where construction vehicles cross.

"Oh look Bod, there's a heavy plant crossing now!" Giggles Min.

Bod and Min are bird watching.

"Hey Min, there's a crane!" Says Bod.

"No Bod it's a heron." Min replies.   "No I'm sure it's a crane." Bod insists.

Bod and Min are watching wildlife today.

Bod can smell the musty scent of a fox. He must be in a fox's territory. "Pooh!" Says Bod not liking the smell.

Min thinks she can hear a woodpecker excavating a nest from a dead tree.

Bod says, "No Min, it's just a woodpecker drumming." On they go again enjoying their day.

It's a lovely calm day. Bod and Min are watching a pair of swans.

"Look Min, that's the male or cob. See how he has a bigger knob at the base of his bill…"

"... and this is the female, or pen." Bod is teaching Min about bird life.

"Oh Bod, does that mean she's his pen friend?" Min giggles.

"I've seen rose coloured swans." Boasts Fox to Bod and Min.

"Oh I've never seen rose-coloured swans!" Answers Min excitedly.

Bod and Min spend the whole day looking but only see the usual white mute swans. They ask Fox…

Fox laughs saying… "Well you get white coloured roses don't you." Bod and Min have been foxed!

Someone has forgotten their doughnut. The delicious smell wafts on the breeze.

Bod finds it. "Hmm. Dooonought." He tries to read.

Like a flash Fox appears. "No, it's dough-nut." Says Fox dribbling all over the bag.

"So do not eat my doughnut." Quips Fox making off with it. "I've been out foxed!" Groans Bod.

"Duck Bod!" Exclaims Min.

Too late. A branch snaps and lands on Bod's head.

"I thought you meant duck as in dinner." Says Bod.
"Me for dinner? You're quackers!" Quacks duck.

"No, I meant duck or grouse." Giggles Min giving him a big consolation lick. Bod feels better now!

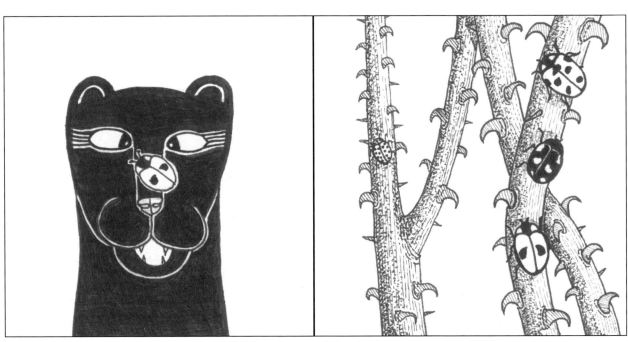

Min tells Bod that whenever she feels homesick, ladybirds always cheer her up.

Oh, how Min loves ladybirds. 7 spots, 2 spots, 22 spots and all the other species.

So the very next time Min feels a little sad…

Bod brings her a ladybird. Er… I don't think he quite understood… Bless!

"Well Min, we've certainly had a good spring and summer." Says Bod thinking back.

But Min is day-dreaming. "Hmm? Spring? Are we going to spring about all day?" She enquires. "Er... no Min." Bod replies.

"Oh. Were you talking about the spring we drink from then?" Enquires Min.

Bod explains he meant the season of spring. "Oh yes! I loved the catkins and caterpillars. Do we get dogkins and dogerpillars as well?" Asks Min. Ah me!

Bod is excited!

He's heard that Sandwich Terns have been spotted near a coastal area not far from them.

"They're only here for the summer and will be heading south soon." Explains Bod.

Sure enough they manage to see a Sandwich Tern. "Gosh yes, that *is* a rare one!" Says Min. Ah me!

A year ago today Bod and Min met. It's their Anniversary. Hooray!

Bod and Min slink off to their lair for a celebration dinner.

"Grrreat chicken surprise but, where's the chicken Min?" Bod calls out to her.

"That's the surprise. There isn't any. We ran out!" Laughs Min. What a catastrophe!

Robin brings Bod and Min a message by special delivery.

Bod and Min are terribly excited. Oh my!

Dear Bod and Min,
Hadn't realised you were both
in England too! I was cast out
as an unwanted pet and now
live on Exmoor. Bit lonely.
Do come and visit. Can't wait
to see you. Best wishes, Your
Cousin, The Beast of Exmoor.

"Who is it from?" Asks Min. "It's from our cousin The Beast of Exmoor. He wants us to visit." Replies Bod.

"Oh yes, let's have a holiday!" Pleads Min. So Bod and Min leave Bodmin Moor and head for Exmoor...

END... Now Epilogue

Epilogue

We have seen Bod evolve from the first storyboards as a real big-cat into a fun cartoon character with his side-kick Min. So, do we have a real population of big-cats here in the British Isles? Well, we know for sure that we do, yet officially the idea remains debatable. Perhaps the cats will be lucky and remain undiscovered thus avoiding persecution and a hunted lifestyle.

Police Wildlife Crime Officers work hard to up hold the law voluntarily where wildlife crime is concerned and C.I.T.E.S (Convention In International Trade In Endangered Species) also do a wonderful job in cracking down on villains. Exotic pets will always run the risk of escaping and individuals that own such pets must take greater responsibility in seeing to it that such escapes do not occur, otherwise not only will the law be broken and the natural balance of our native flora and fauna upset but, it is totally inhumane and unfair on the creatures concerned.

So what of Bod and Min? Well, now they will slowly make their way out of Bodmin Moor and head for Exmoor via Dartmoor to meet their cousin The Beast of Exmoor. Who knows what they will get up to along the way. Watch this space…

Endymion Beer FZS MBOU